Original title:
Resonance of Relationships

Author: Sabrina Sarvik
ISBN HARDBACK: 978-9916-86-800-3
ISBN PAPERBACK: 978-9916-86-801-0
ISBN EBOOK: 978-9916-86-802-7

Heartstrings in Harmony

In twilight's glow we gently sway,
With whispers soft that guide our way.
Two souls entwined, a sweet embrace,
In every heartbeat, love we trace.

The stars above, they twinkle bright,
As melodies unfold each night.
The rhythm of our dreams align,
In perfect time, your heart with mine.

Through storms that rage and winds that howl,
We'll find our peace, in love we'll prowl.
With every tear, a laugh will bloom,
Together we dispel the gloom.

In moments shared, we dare to dance,
Each glance a spark, a fleeting chance.
Together we compose the tune,
In whispered hopes beneath the moon.

So hand in hand, we'll forge ahead,
With every word and thought we've said.
For in this life, our hearts will sing,
In harmony, true love will bring.

The Thread That Connects

In silence woven, soft and light,
A thread unites both day and night.
With gentle pulls, it starts to blend,
A bond of love that will not end.

Through trials faced and joys we share,
Each moment smooths our every care.
An unseen force, yet oh so real,
A sacred bond, a soothing reel.

Heartstrings in Concert

In harmony, two souls collide,
Like melodies that cannot hide.
A symphony that's played with grace,
Each note reflects our warm embrace.

With every beat, the rhythm grows,
In whispered tones, affection flows.
A dance of hearts that intertwine,
In concert sweet, your hand in mine.

Reflections of Us

In mirrors clear, our stories glow,
A canvas bright where love can flow.
Each laughter shared, a brush of light,
Reflected in the starry night.

Together we create a scene,
Of dreams fulfilled and spaces seen.
In every glance, a truth unfolds,
A timeless tale that love beholds.

The Dance of Affection

Upon the floor, we spin and sway,
In gentle steps, we find our way.
A rhythm sparks, our spirits rise,
As heartbeat echoes soft replies.

In every turn, a story told,
A dance of warmth that won't grow cold.
With love's embrace, we glide in sync,
Two souls entwined, we never shrink.

Echoes of Togetherness

In the silence, we reside,
Shared glances, hearts open wide.
In laughter's glow, our spirits soar,
Together we are, forevermore.

Through storms we stand, hands entwined,
In memories sweet, our joy we find.
With every beat, our songs unite,
In darkest hours, we bring the light.

Whispers Across Time

In the twilight, secrets blend,
Echoes of stories that never end.
History speaks in subtle tones,
Binding our hearts, like ancient stones.

Footsteps linger on dusty trails,
While dreams dance softly, like gentle gales.
Moments suspended, like stars in night,
Together we weave, our shared delight.

Bonds Beyond Measure

With every hug, a promise made,
Through tears and joy, our lives displayed.
Unseen ties that bond our fate,
In silence, we find what words can't state.

Paths may diverge, yet souls remain,
In laughter and love, we'll bear the strain.
Through trials fierce, our roots run deep,
In endless nights, together we leap.

Harmony in Dissonance

In chaos found, we learn to sing,
Notes of discord can still bring spring.
From varied hues, a canvas grows,
In every clash, a beauty flows.

With every storm, a chance to mend,
Through disarray, our voices blend.
In fractured tunes, we find the way,
Together we rise, come what may.

Echoes of Affection

In the quiet dusk, love calls,
Gentle whispers softly fall.
Memories linger in the air,
A bond that time cannot impair.

Moments shared, laughter rings,
As the heart in unison sings.
Each glance, a promise made,
In this dance, we won't fade.

Through the storms and skies so clear,
Our affection conquers fear.
With every heartbeat, we unite,
Guided by the stars at night.

Time may pass, but love will last,
Echoes of affection, unsurpassed.
In the tapestry of our days,
Together we'll find endless ways.

Hand in hand, we journey on,
In the light of every dawn.
Your laughter still, my sweetest song,
In this symphony, we belong.

Threads of Togetherness

Stitched with love, our lives entwine,
Each thread a story, richly divine.
Through the fabric, warmth does flow,
In this embrace, we gently grow.

The colors bright, the patterns bold,
Each moment shared, a treasure to hold.
In every fold, a memory lies,
Beneath the vast and open skies.

Woven tightly, yet free to soar,
Together, we can face much more.
In laughter’s thread and sorrow's seam,
We stitch the fabric of our dream.

Across the years, our tapestry spreads,
Comforting as each other’s threads.
With every sun and every moon,
Together, dear, we find our tune.

As seasons change and time moves free,
Threads of togetherness bind you and me.
In every stitch, our love's embrace,
A masterpiece in time and space.

Whispering Hearts

In the twilight's softest glow,
Whispering hearts in gentle flow.
Secrets shared beneath the stars,
In a world that's truly ours.

Promises glimmer, softly spoken,
In every word, love's unbroken.
Breathless moments, moments rare,
In the silence, we both care.

Softly tickling, the night breeze plays,
Caressing dreams in tender ways.
A glance ignites, a spark ignites,
Whispering hearts on endless nights.

Through every trial, side by side,
With whispering hearts, love won't hide.
Together we stand, together we dream,
In each other's eyes, a radiant gleam.

We'll dance through life, hand in hand,
Fate intertwined, a perfect strand.
Whispering hearts, forever free,
In this beautiful harmony.

Lost in Translation

Words slip away like whispers,
Fleeting thoughts in the air.
Meanings change like shadows,
Leaving hearts unaware.

A smile can hold a secret,
While silence speaks in tones.
Lost in a sea of phrases,
We wander far from home.

Eyes try to find the answer,
But the heart knows the truth.
In every awkward moment,
Lies the ghost of our youth.

Thoughts drift like paper boats,
On a river of lost dreams.
Each conversation a voyage,
Through mended, frayed seams.

Yet in the space unspoken,
Connections start to glow.
For even when we're distant,
Love can still overflow.

Layers of Laughter

Laughter dances through the room,
Like sunlight through the trees.
Layered tones of joy and jest,
A symphony of ease.

In every shared moment, bright,
A chuckle, a warm glance.
Each layer peels like petals,
In our playful, simple dance.

Sounding deep like music chords,
It warms the coldest heart.
In laughter's warm embrace, we find,
A bond that won't depart.

Through giggles and soft whispers,
We craft our secret ties.
In layers rich as stories,
Our friendship never dies.

Each chuckle has a meaning,
Wrapped in stories we unfold.
Laughter holds our memories,
In a tapestry of gold.

The Canvas of Communication

Words are strokes on canvas,
Painting thoughts so bold.
Colors blend in harmony,
Stories to be told.

Silence holds a whisper,
A brush with gentle care.
Each heartbeat an expression,
In the gallery we share.

Textures of connection,
In every glance we give.
Our spirits intertwining,
In the art of how we live.

With every rise and fall,
Conversations create art.
Brushes dance like shadows,
Revealing every heart.

In the gallery of moments,
Colors collide and blend.
The canvas is our journey,
Where messages transcend.

Bridges of Belonging

Bridges rise from common dreams,
Arching over the divide.
Connection grows in laughter,
Where hearts can safely hide.

Hand in hand through stormy weather,
We walk the winding ways.
In unity, we discover,
A thousand shared days.

Every smile builds a pathway,
Every word lays a stone.
Together we are stronger,
Never standing alone.

In the warmth of shared stories,
We find our hearts align.
Building bridges of belonging,
Where love can intertwine.

Through the echoes of our voices,
We share what is so real.
Together, we are a family,
Unbreakable, we heal.

In the Chord of Hearts

In the silence, secrets lie,
Whispers drift, a soft goodbye.
Every heartbeat sings its tune,
Binding souls beneath the moon.

Strings of fate entwined so tight,
Warm embraces, tender light.
Yearning glances, unconfessed,
Love's sweet song, forever blessed.

Time may fade, but feelings stay,
In the dance, we find our way.
Chords of laughter, tears that start,
Echo softly in the heart.

Notes of joy and pain we share,
Echoes linger in the air.
Harmony in all we do,
In this rhythm, me and you.

Set the stage for whispered vows,
In the quiet, love avows.
Together we shall face the night,
In the chord, our hearts take flight.

Unspoken Agreements

In the gaze, a pact unfolds,
Silent truths that need not be told.
Hands entwined, no words required,
In this space, our souls are wired.

Moments pause, the world stands still,
In shared breaths, we find our will.
Glimmers of trust fill the room,
Unseen ties begin to bloom.

Promises forged in gentle light,
In shadows cast, we find our sight.
Every nod, a vow assured,
In this bond, we are secured.

Lingering at the edge of dreams,
In every glance, the future seems.
A dance without a single word,
In the silence, love is stirred.

Through the tides, we find our way,
Unyielding bonds that softly sway.
In the quiet, truths are known,
In unison, we are home.

Melodies of Memory

Fleeting notes of days gone by,
Whispers soft, a fleeting sigh.
In the corners of the mind,
Melodies of love intertwined.

Ticking clocks and laughter’s ring,
Past reflections softly sing.
Echoed joys, a bittersweet,
In the rhythm, shadows meet.

Chasing dreams like butterflies,
In the heart, a hope that flies.
Fragments of a sweet refrain,
In the tapestry of pain.

Harmonies that time can't sever,
Moments cherished, lost forever.
With each chord, a story told,
In our hearts, the memories hold.

Through the years, we find our song,
In the dance of right and wrong.
Melodies that never fade,
In the silence, love's parade.

Shadows of Intimacy

In the twilight, shadows creep,
Secrets shared, no need for sleep.
In the darkness, we confide,
In this trust, our fears subside.

Fingers trace on skin so bare,
Breathless sighs hang in the air.
Soft caresses, whispers low,
In this space, love’s embers glow.

Glimmering dreams beneath the stars,
Locked in time, no distant bars.
Each heartbeat echoes in the night,
Shadows dance, love takes flight.

In the stillness, hearts collide,
With every touch, our souls abide.
Bound together, never apart,
In the shadows, we restart.

Through the veil, we seek and find,
Entwined futures, hearts aligned.
In the whispers, love's decree,
In the shadows, we are free.

Flights of Fancy

In skies where dreams take flight,
Whispers of the stars ignite.
Wings of hope, we soar so high,
Chasing clouds that drift on by.

With every gust, we twist and turn,
The heart's delight, a flame that burns.
In the dance of wind and grace,
We find our truth in endless space.

Each feathered thought, a spark of light,
Guiding us through the velvet night.
Boundless realms of limitless views,
Every moment, we choose to muse.

Landing softly on dreams once sown,
In this vast sky, we are not alone.
Together we tread on paths unknown,
In flights of fancy, we've brightly grown.

Portraits of Partnership

Two hearts paint a canvas bright,
Side by side, in day and night.
Each brush stroke, a bond so true,
Creating life’s vibrant hue.

In laughter shared and secrets kept,
Through storms we've faced, and tears we've wept.
Your hand in mine, we stand as one,
A portrait drawn, our days begun.

Every challenge, a shade of gray,
Yet in unity, we find our way.
With quiet strength, our roots entwine,
In every moment, your heart is mine.

Together we rise, we dance, we dream,
In every look, in every gleam.
Through life's lens, our love's displayed,
In portraits of partnership, forever made.

Fragments of Forever

In fleeting moments, life unfolds,
Whispers of memories gently hold.
Fragments of forever, soft and clear,
Carved in time, forever near.

Each laugh, a treasure we can claim,
Each tear, a flicker of passion's flame.
In every heartbeat, echoes reside,
In shadows of time, love won't hide.

We stitch our stories with threads of gold,
In the tapestry of time, legends told.
With every sunrise, a page anew,
In fragments, our love breaks through.

Moments like stars, they guide our way,
Lighting up the night, at the end of day.
In every glance, eternity glows,
In fragments of forever, our garden grows.

Threads of Time

In the loom of life, we weave our fate,
Each thread a story, we contemplate.
Colors of joy, shadows of pain,
In the fabric of time, we remain.

Moments entwined, like silk and lace,
Fragile yet strong, in love’s embrace.
Each twist and turn, a lesson learned,
With every fiber, our hearts are stirred.

Through years that pass, and seasons change,
In our hearts' quilt, nothing feels strange.
The threads connect us, near and far,
In the tapestry of life, just as we are.

As time unfolds, we cherish each seam,
Binding our dreams, a radiant beam.
In threads of time, we find our rhyme,
Together we are, forever in prime.

Choreography of Trust

In the rhythm of our hearts, we sway,
Bound by promises, come what may.
Steps entwined, we dance through night,
In every glance, a shared delight.

Fingers trace the path we take,
In gentle moves, no hearts to break.
Whispers in the dark, we share,
In silence found, a truth laid bare.

With every twirl, we rise anew,
Building hopes, our dreams in view.
A trust so deep, it knows no end,
In every beat, my heart, my friend.

So let us dance, through joy and strife,
A choreography that shapes our life.
Together we flow, a graceful trust,
In harmony we bloom, in love we must.

Notes in the Silence

In moments hushed, where whispers cease,
Ears tune in to a subtle peace.
Between the sounds, a story glows,
In empty spaces, wisdom flows.

Each breath we take, a note it sings,
Like gentle winds brushing wings.
In quietude, our spirits soar,
Finding meaning in what's before.

Unspoken words, like shadows dance,
In silence, we discover chance.
A melody of unvoiced truth,
In calm reflections, we find our youth.

So let us listen to the still,
To the heartbeats, its rhythmic thrill.
In silence, notes of life unite,
Creating harmony, pure and bright.

The Spirit of Affinity

In gentle bonds, our spirits blend,
A connection deep, it won’t suspend.
Shared laughter echoes through the air,
In unity, we find our care.

Through every storm, we hold on tight,
Guiding each other towards the light.
Two souls as one, a harmony formed,
In the warmth of love, we are warmed.

A journey walked hand in hand,
In the understanding, we firmly stand.
Our hearts aligned, a common thread,
In the tapestry of trust, we are led.

So let the spirit of affinity bloom,
In its embrace, there’s no room for gloom.
A bond unbreakable, strong and true,
In every heartbeat, I cherish you.

A Tapestry of Emotions

In colors bright, our feelings weave,
A tapestry that we conceive.
Threads of joy and shades of pain,
Together they dance in love's refrain.

Each stitch a memory, rich and deep,
In silent moments, we often keep.
Love's vibrant hues, a canvas wide,
Where laughter and sorrow coincide.

In every knot, a lesson learned,
Through passion's fire, our spirits burned.
Embracing all that life bestows,
In the fabric of time, our spirit grows.

So let us create, with heart and hand,
A tapestry woven, where we stand.
In every fiber, our essence glows,
In this artful life, together we chose.

Silhouettes of Support

In shadows cast by evening light,
We stand together, ready to fight.
With whispers soft, we share our fears,
A bond of trust that calms our tears.

Through storms that rage and winds that howl,
Your hand in mine, we brave the foul.
Together we rise, together we fall,
In silhouettes, we hear the call.

With every step, our hearts align,
In silent strength, our souls entwine.
Through darkest nights, our spirits soar,
In every glance, we're so much more.

As dawn breaks bright, we see the way,
With every hope, we seize the day.
In shadows deep, we find our light,
Silhouettes of love, forever bright.

Pathways of Passion

Through winding roads where dreams take flight,
We chase the stars, igniting the night.
With every heartbeat, every sigh,
Our passions dance, they reach the sky.

In whispered winds, our secrets weave,
A tapestry that makes us believe.
With every step, our spirits blend,
On pathways bright, love knows no end.

With colors bold, our journey unfolds,
In tales of fire, our hearts behold.
As seasons change, we stand our ground,
In passion's arms, we're forever bound.

Through valleys deep and mountains high,
In joy and pain, we learn to fly.
With every glance, our futures meet,
On pathways paved, our love's complete.

Fragrance of Familiarity

In every smile, a scent so sweet,
The warmth of home beneath our feet.
Through gentle hugs and laughter pure,
In love's embrace, we feel secure.

With every breath, the memories rise,
Like blossoms blooming 'neath the skies.
In scents of vanilla, coffee's brew,
The fragrance wraps us, strong and true.

Through cherished moments, time stands still,
In quiet corners, our hearts fulfill.
With every heartbeat, every sigh,
The fragrance lingers, you and I.

In twilight's hush, the past remains,
In whispers soft, love's sweet refrains.
In familiarity, we find our peace,
A fragrant bond that will not cease.

Synchronized Souls

In harmony where rhythms play,
Our souls unite in every sway.
With every beat, we find our song,
In synchronized steps, we belong.

Through silence shared, our thoughts collide,
In gentle glances, hearts confide.
With every twirl, a dance so free,
In unison, just you and me.

With laughter bright, we fill the air,
In perfect cadence, love's sweet flair.
With every pause, our spirits meet,
In synchronized time, life feels complete.

As twilight falls, we remain bright,
Two stars entwined, a glowing sight.
In every moment, we find our role,
In synchronized hearts, we are whole.

Notes of Nostalgia

In the quiet of the night,
Memories softly play,
Whispers of laughter echo,
In shadows of yesterday.

Faded pictures bring back,
A warmth we can't forget,
Moments dance like fireflies,
In the glow of sunset.

Pages turned with care,
Ink stains on my hand,
Every line a story,
From a distant land.

Time slips through our fingers,
Yet holds us close in dreams,
Each note a gentle heartbeat,
Always bursting at the seams.

With each passing season,
The past sings to me still,
Guiding my heart gently,
As I wander at will.

Reflected Flame

In the stillness of twilight,
I see your spark in the dark,
A flicker of memories,
Igniting an enduring mark.

Beneath the weary sky,
Your eyes hold a glow,
Reflected in the silence,
A warmth only we know.

Echoes of laughter ring,
In the shadows we chase,
A dance of flickering light,
In this infinite space.

With every whispered promise,
A flame begins to grow,
Drawing us closer still,
In the night's tender flow.

A bond that never flickers,
Through storms and quiet rain,
Together we're unbroken,
In this reflected flame.

The Map of Us

Drawn with lines of laughter,
And ink of shared dreams,
The roads we've traveled,
Flow like gentle streams.

From mountains to oceans,
Each place holds a tale,
A compass that guides us,
Through every wind and gale.

Marked by starlit evenings,
And dawn's rosy hue,
Every step a memory,
In the map of me and you.

Navigating together,
Through thick and through thin,
Each journey a treasure,
With you, I always win.

As we chart the unknown,
With love as our guide,
The map of us unfolds,
With every stride.

Clarity in Connection

In the noise of the world,
Your voice cuts like a knife,
A beacon of true meaning,
Illuminating life.

Eyes meet across the distance,
A silence speaks so loud,
In the depths of our hearts,
We stand unbowed, proud.

Truth rests in our gazes,
Where words may often fail,
In a bond unbroken,
We set our own sail.

Through the clutter and chaos,
Your presence is a balm,
A soothing, gentle whisper,
In the storm, a calm.

In the tapestry we weave,
Each thread tells a tale,
A clarity in connection,
Where love will never pale.

The Symphony of Souls

In the quiet of the night,
Each heart plays its tune,
Melodies softly intertwine,
Underneath the silver moon.

Whispers float on the breeze,
Carried from soul to soul,
Harmony that brings us peace,
Together we are whole.

Notes that dance through the dark,
Painting dreams with each sound,
A story in every spark,
In this symphony profound.

With every pulse, we rise,
Echoes of joy and pain,
In life's grand enterprise,
We find sunshine in the rain.

As the final chord fades,
We cherish what remains,
The bond that never wades,
In memories, love reigns.

Ripples of Emotion

A drop in the still pond,
Sends waves to the shore,
Emotions stretch and bond,
Gently asking for more.

Laughter breaks through the calm,
A cascade of delight,
While sorrow, like a balm,
Wraps us in its soft night.

Tears fall like gentle rain,
Creating circles wide,
Each ripple holds the pain,
Of the hearts that confide.

In whispers of the heart,
We share our hidden fears,
But through it, we impart,
The strength to face our years.

So let the water flow,
With every joy and strife,
For in these ripples grow,
The depths of our shared life.

Portraits of Together

Canvas stretched and pristine,
Brush strokes wild with grace,
In colors brightly seen,
We paint our own embrace.

Each portrait tells a tale,
Of moments intertwined,
In laughter or in pale,
Expressions undefined.

The hues of joy and pain,
Mix in a vibrant blur,
In shadows we remain,
Yet always, love's the spur.

Frames adorned with our dreams,
Captured through years gone by,
With sunlight's gentle beams,
Reflecting who am I.

Together in this art,
We forge a world anew,
With every beat, each heart,
Our masterpieces grew.

Fragments of Us

Scattered like autumn leaves,
Each piece tells a story,
In silence, the heart grieves,
Yet finds its hidden glory.

Moments broken and whole,
Time we cannot retrieve,
Yet, in each little soul,
Lies the strength to believe.

Shards of laughter and tears,
We gather and we mend,
Through all our fleeting years,
We learn how to descend.

In the mosaic of life,
Beauty hides in the cracks,
With hope that ends the strife,
And love that never lacks.

So let us stand as one,
In this fragile embrace,
For in the setting sun,
We find our sacred space.

Collective Heartbeats

In the quiet dusk, we gather close,
Echoes of laughter, a gentle prose.
Each heartbeat syncs, a rhythmic song,
Together in moments, where we belong.

Through shadows cast by the setting sun,
Hearts intertwined, we are never done.
With every breath, a silent vow,
In unity, we find our now.

Whispers linger in the cool night air,
Stories exchanged, memories to share.
A pulse of warmth beneath the stars,
Reminders that love can heal all scars.

In dreams we dance, a tender glow,
Through winding paths, together we grow.
Collective heartbeats, our guiding light,
In this harmony, we take flight.

Imprints of Togetherness

Under the moon, our shadows blend,
In every footprint, a story penned.
Hand in hand, we walk this line,
Every moment a sacred sign.

Through fields of gold, we take our time,
Each laugh, each tear, a perfect rhyme.
Imprints soft on this earthen floor,
Together we've opened every door.

Bright eyes reflect a shared delight,
In every touch, the world feels right.
Through stormy skies or weathered gales,
Our bonds remain, through all life’s trails.

With every word, a bridge we build,
In silent peace, our hearts are filled.
Imprints of love, like stars at night,
Forever glistening, pure and bright.

The Language of Touch

Fingers brush against the skin,
Silent gestures where we begin.
In quiet moments, desires unfold,
The language of touch, tender and bold.

A glance exchanged, a soft embrace,
In every movement, we find our place.
Whispers of warmth in the still, cool air,
Hands entwined, a promise to care.

Through gentle caress and fleeting feels,
In this dance, our fate reveals.
Unspoken words wrapped in a sigh,
Together we rise, together we fly.

In every heartbeat, connection's grace,
Through layers of time, we leave our trace.
The language of touch speaks loud and clear,
A melody only we can hear.

Tender Traces

In the afterglow of shared dreams,
We find ourselves in soft sunbeams.
Tender traces on the canvas of time,
Through simple moments, a gentle rhyme.

Silent promises linger in the breeze,
Our spirits dance, like leaves on trees.
With every laugh, with every sigh,
Together we weave, you and I.

In the quiet corners of the heart,
Every touch, a work of art.
Each shared glance, a story told,
In the warmth of love, we unfold.

Through storms and calm, we journey on,
Creating paths, from dusk till dawn.
Tender traces, soft and light,
A journey together, our souls ignite.

Chords of Companionship

In the melody of laughter,
We find solace and cheer.
Together we strum life's guitar,
Notes ringing sweet and clear.

Through trials and the rain,
We play our hearts' refrain.
Each moment, a vibrant chord,
In harmonious accord.

With hands intertwined, we stand,
Creating our own band.
Every song a memory,
In perfect symphony.

The echoes of our stories,
Resonate in soft light.
Through every minor key,
We build our shared delight.

In the quiet of the night,
Our friendship still holds tight.
Forever tuned in love,
A bond that soars above.

The Silence Between Us

In the hush of the evening,
We find peace in the still.
Words aren't always needed,
Our hearts, they know the will.

Glimmers of understanding,
Twinkling in our eyes.
The silence speaks its truth,
Beneath the starlit skies.

With every quiet moment,
We weave a tapestry.
Of trust and shared intentions,
In perfect harmony.

Whispers of unspoken thoughts,
Linger in the air.
In the comfort of your presence,
I feel your loving care.

The distance of no words,
Can be a bond so tight.
Our souls dance in silence,
In the soft glow of night.

Notes from the Heart

In every pulse that beats,
A melody begins.
Notes that flow like rivers,
Where love and life begins.

The whispers of affection,
Are songs that never fade.
Each heartbeat a reminder,
Of the joy that you've made.

With every laugh and tear,
We compose our sweet refrain.
Through the rhythm of our days,
Our connection, like a chain.

In the symphony of us,
Every note is true.
The chorus of our moments,
Always leads back to you.

So let the music play,
In the fabric of our lives.
With every note and measure,
Together, love thrives.

Shared Frequencies

In the air between us,
Vibrations dance and sway.
We tune into each heartbeat,
In a beautiful array.

Echoes of our laughter,
Resound through every room.
Our spirits intertwining,
Like flowers in full bloom.

With every conversation,
We find our favorite tune.
In the harmony of friendship,
We rise like the moon.

Through waves of understanding,
We navigate the night.
Our shared frequencies blend,
In the glow of warm light.

The music of our bond,
Plays softly in our hearts.
Together we are stronger,
As each new day starts.

Intervals of Intimacy

In whispers soft, our secrets sway,
Like shadows dancing, night to day.
Fleeting glances, hearts embrace,
In sacred spaces, time's sweet trace.

A touch that lingers, light as air,
Connected souls, a gentle pair.
We share the silence, breaths in tune,
Underneath the watchful moon.

With laughter shared, we bridge the gap,
In tender moments, let love unwrap.
Each heartbeat echoes, rich and deep,
Through intervals of dreams we keep.

Like tides that rise, then fall away,
Our bond remains, come what may.
In fleeting hours, eternity flows,
In intervals, true intimacy grows.

Holding close, we find our way,
Silent promises that softly play.
A symphony of heartbeats near,
Intervals of love, forever dear.

Secrets in the Silence

In the quiet, voices blend,
Softly tucked, where secrets mend.
Glimpses caught in knowing eyes,
In silence, truth and heart arise.

Words unspoken, heavy air,
Each breath shared, a silent prayer.
Moments linger, deep and vast,
In the silence, shadows cast.

Echoes whisper through the night,
Hidden tales in fading light.
In every pause, a tale untold,
Secrets wrapped in silence bold.

Conversations without sound,
In the stillness, love is found.
A precious bond that speaks so clear,
Secrets in the silence near.

Glimmers of hope in quiet souls,
Where unvoiced dreams begin to roll.
With every heartbeat, trust defends,
In silence shared, the journey bends.

Lattice of Love

In tangled threads our lives entwined,
Weaving dreams, our hearts aligned.
A lattice forms, so strong, so true,
Cradling hopes, me and you.

Each moment shared, a story spun,
In laughter's light, we come undone.
Through trials faced, we find our way,
A tapestry of love each day.

With woven colors, bright and bold,
Our intertwined paths, a story told.
In gentle strength, we support each other,
A lattice built, like no other.

Through storms that pass and sun that shines,
We cultivate what love defines.
In every notch, a place to grow,
A lattice of love, steady flow.

Each thread a memory, rich and fine,
In this design, your heart entwines.
Together strong, we shall rise above,
Everlasting is this lattice of love.

The Weight of Words

Words can linger, heavy as stone,
In shared moments, seeds are sown.
The weight of silence, a tender bind,
In every phrase, intent to find.

Each syllable carries, floods and tides,
In whispered truths, the heart confides.
A choice of language, sharp and sweet,
The weight of words, our souls complete.

In careless speech, a wound can bloom,
While gentle whispers, chase the gloom.
The echoes linger, in the air,
The weight of words, beyond compare.

With careful thought, we choose our lines,
Each statement crafted, like fine wines.
In loving tones, we build and mend,
The weight of words, our voices blend.

From thoughts to heart, they bridge the space,
In every uttered line, a trace.
Together we converse, hearts in chord,
Forever bound by the weight of words.

Silent Conversations

In the quiet, whispers flow,
Eyes speak a language we both know.
Time stands still, in shadows cast,
Moments linger, futures past.

Breathes intertwine, hearts in sync,
Silent nods, no need to think.
A universe inside each gaze,
Lost in thoughts, in muted haze.

Words unspoken, heavy yet light,
In the dark, we share our light.
The space between, a sacred trust,
In silence, we find what's just.

Echoes of laughter, soft and true,
Each glance a promise, made for two.
We build a world, brick by brick,
In silent conversations, love's little flick.

Time may fade, yet here we stand,
Together weaving dreams so grand.
In the stillness, we both belong,
Silent conversations, our endless song.

Ties That Bind and Break

Through laughter shared, our bond was strong,
In tangled fates, we learned to belong.
Promises made, tied with a thread,
Yet whispers of doubt, still widely spread.

Moments cherished, we danced in the rain,
But storms soon came, bringing the pain.
With every tear, the distance grew,
An unraveling knot, no longer true.

Holding tight, we tried to mend,
But fragile ties that twist and bend.
Love's tapestry, worn and frayed,
In shadows cast, our colors fade.

A spark remained, deep in our core,
Yet echoes linger of tales of yore.
With every breath, we learned to fight,
The ties that bind, now took their flight.

In memories held, the warmth remains,
For love that binds can also bring chains.
Though we may wander, paths diverged,
In hearts, forever, we'll be submerged.

Frequencies of Love

In waves that crash, a heartbeat finds,
The rhythm flows, two souls aligned.
Melodies drift through time and space,
In frequencies, we find our place.

Notes so soft, a gentle tune,
We dance beneath the silver moon.
Harmonics rise, the music plays,
In every glance, our spirit sways.

Vibrations strong, like summer's breeze,
Our laughter echoes through the trees.
In every hug, a silent song,
Frequencies where we both belong.

Syncopated beats in lover's embrace,
A tranquil pulse, a sacred space.
Together we weave our sound so pure,
In this symphony of hearts, we're sure.

With every chord, our story's spun,
In frequencies of love, we are one.
Through highs and lows, we rise above,
Together forever, in waves of love.

The Language of Touch

Fingers trace where words do fail,
In gentle strokes, our hearts unveil.
A brush of skin, electric thrill,
In silence speaks, the heart's own will.

With every squeeze, a promise made,
In warm embraces, fears allayed.
The warmth of hands, our stories blend,
In the language of touch, we transcend.

From soft caress to fierce embrace,
In every tender, sacred space.
Communicating without a sound,
Where mutual solace can be found.

In moments shared, a world unfolds,
Secrets whispered, warmth and gold.
We are in sync, our souls ignite,
The language of touch feels so right.

A simple gesture, yet so profound,
In every heartbeat, love is found.
In tactile whispers, our spirits soar,
In the language of touch, forevermore.

Flickering Flames

In the dark, they dance bright,
Whispers in the quiet night.
Each spark tells a tale anew,
Glowing embers, orange and blue.

Memories lose their weight,
As they flicker, they create.
Moments lost but never far,
Guided by a distant star.

With warmth that time can't steal,
They remind us how to feel.
Softly calling, they embrace,
Illuminating every space.

In the breeze, they softly sway,
Fueling dreams that drift away.
With every pulse, they seem to know,
The heart's tender, glowing throe.

So let them burn, let them shine,
Each flame a story, yours and mine.
Together in this radiant glow,
We'll find our way, we'll always know.

Hand in Hand

Two souls meet on life's grand stage,
Together turning every page.
With fingers intertwined tight,
They face the world, hearts full of light.

Through stormy skies and sunny days,
In every laugh, in every gaze.
They find strength in gentle touch,
Together, they can do so much.

When shadows fall and doubts arise,
They stand firm, never compromise.
With whispered words and softest sighs,
They lift each other to the skies.

In silence shared, a bond so deep,
Secrets cherished, promises keep.
A dance of trust, a love so grand,
Two lives now woven, hand in hand.

So here they walk, through thick and thin,
A journey where love will always win.
For side by side, they take the stand,
Facing life, hand in hand.

Waves of Understanding

Gentle tides can soothe the soul,
In their rhythm, we find whole.
With each wave that rolls ashore,
Whispers of wisdom, evermore.

Beneath the surface, secrets hide,
Life's lessons flow with the tide.
A dance of currents, ebb and flow,
In their depths, we come to know.

As oceans rise and fall in grace,
We learn to cherish every place.
In stillness and in stormy seas,
Understanding comes, like the breeze.

Together, we sail through the night,
Navigating with love as our light.
Every wave brings us a chance,
To share the gift of life’s vast dance.

So let us ride this ocean’s crest,
Finding peace and love, our quest.
With every wave, we'll understand,
In this journey, hand in hand.

The Fabric of Us

Threads entwined, vivid and bright,
Woven closely, day and night.
In every stitch, a story told,
The fabric of us, a sight to hold.

With colors vibrant, tones anew,
Each moment adds to our view.
Embroidered dreams, sewn with care,
A tapestry rich, beyond compare.

In softer tones, we find our peace,
In tangled threads, we seek release.
Through joy and sorrow, thread the seams,
We cultivate our hopes and dreams.

Resilient fabric, strong and wide,
Cradling thoughts we cannot hide.
Together we mend, together we grow,
The fabric of us, a steady flow.

So let us cherish every hue,
For in this weave, it's me and you.
Through every twist and turn we trust,
In this beautiful, shared fabric of us.

Love's Lullabies

In whispers soft like evening mist,
Our hearts entwined with tender bliss.
The stars above begin to glow,
As dreams of us begin to flow.

With every sigh, a story spun,
In moonlit nights, we are as one.
The melody of love we sing,
A gentle touch that makes us wing.

In shadows deep, your voice I find,
A quiet strength that soothes the mind.
Through trials faced and laughter shared,
Our lullabies show how much we cared.

So let the night embrace our dreams,
Where love is more than just it seems.
In every heartbeat, softly played,
A symphony of love conveyed.

With every dawn, new hopes arise,
Our hearts echo beneath the skies.
In love's embrace, we find our peace,
A lullaby that will not cease.

Eclipsed Emotions

In shadows cast by fleeting light,
I glimpse the truth, obscured from sight.
Your laughter rings like distant bells,
Yet in my heart, a silence dwells.

A fleeting smile, a whispered sigh,
The moments come, then quickly fly.
A tapestry of joy and pain,
Our love eclipsed, though much remains.

Within your gaze, a stormy sea,
Waves crashing soft, yet drowning me.
An endless dance of dark and bright,
The shadows pull us from the light.

Yet still I search for rays of hope,
To pull us from this shaded slope.
Though tangled feelings blur the way,
I'll find the truth, come what may.

In this eclipse, we'll stand so tall,
For love can conquer shadows' thrall.
With every breath, I'll reach for you,
And face the dark to find what's true.

The Space Between Heartbeats

In quietude, the stillness breathes,
A moment held, where time retrieves.
The space between each heartbeat's song,
Is where our souls have learned to belong.

A fragile pause, a whispered prayer,
In silence, love blooms everywhere.
We linger in this sacred hush,
Embracing life in every rush.

With every pulse, a world unfolds,
Vast stories shared, and secrets told.
In each heartbeat, memories dance,
A timeless waltz, a sweet romance.

The space we share, a sacred bond,
Connected hearts, of which I'm fond.
Through every breath, we find our way,
As night gives in to break of day.

So let the beat of hearts align,
A rhythm found, a perfect sign.
In this embrace, forever stay,
In love’s pure light, we’ll find our way.

Mosaics of Memory

In pieces small, our moments gleam,
A tapestry, a waking dream.
Each memory, a shard of light,
Reflecting joy, and even fright.

With every laugh, a color bright,
With every tear, a shade of night.
We gather all, both dark and fair,
Creating art, a love to share.

In frames of time, our stories weave,
From countless threads, we dare believe.
A mosaic made of joys and sorrow,
Each piece a promise for tomorrow.

With gentle hands, we shape our past,
Through every storm, together fast.
In fragments, find the whole anew,
For love's mosaic is made of you.

So let us cherish each small part,
For in our lives, we find the heart.
A masterpiece of love portrayed,
In every hue that life has laid.

The Groove of Growth

In the soil, roots entwine,
Seeds of hope, a life divine.
Beneath the sun, they stretch and strive,
Nature's dance, we come alive.

Through the seasons, blooms reveal,
Tender whispers, hearts that heal.
In the rain, we find our spark,
Gentle guidance through the dark.

From the small to grand delight,
Every step ignites our light.
In the journey, we discover,
Strength in all, and love for others.

Branches reaching for the sky,
Every leaf, a silent sigh.
In the shade, our dreams ignite,
Growing stronger in our plight.

With each moment, we embrace,
All the changes we must face.
In the groove of endless growth,
Feel the bond, and hold it close.

Echoes of Embrace

In the twilight's gentle glow,
Whispers soft, like winds that blow.
Hearts connect, a timeless hum,
In each echo, we become.

Through the laughter, through the tears,
All our hopes and hidden fears.
In the silence, love resounds,
Familiar touch in subtle sounds.

Every heartbeat tells a tale,
Through the storms, we will not fail.
Holding tight when shadows fall,
In your arms, I've found my all.

With each memory we share,
In your presence, nothing compares.
Echoes linger in the night,
Guiding us with softest light.

Together wrapped in love's embrace,
Every moment, sacred space.
In the dance of life's sweet chase,
We find solace in this place.

Unspoken Understandings

In the quiet, glances plead,
Shared moments plant the seed.
Through the words we left unsaid,
Lies the truth where hearts are led.

In the stillness, feelings grow,
Silent knowing, we both know.
Every sigh and every glance,
Tells a story, shares a dance.

Through the chaos, we unite,
In the shadows, find the light.
With our souls, we intertwine,
In the silence, love will shine.

In the warmth of someone's eye,
Words unspoken never die.
In the spaces in between,
Lies a bond that's rarely seen.

Through the storms and distant lands,
In unspoken, love still stands.
Feel the pulse of what we share,
Beyond words, we're always there.

The Rhythm of Radiance

In the morning light we rise,
Chasing dreams beneath the skies.
With each heartbeat, hope's embrace,
Feel the warmth, the softest grace.

Every moment, bright and bold,
In our stories, truths unfold.
Watch the colors paint the day,
With the rhythm, we will sway.

In the laughter, joy ignites,
Shining through our darkest nights.
With each step, we make our mark,
Together lighting up the dark.

Through the cadence of our song,
Frozen moments, we belong.
In the dance of life's parade,
Every heartbeat, love conveyed.

As the stars light up the sky,
Feel the pulse that will not die.
In the rhythm of life's chance,
We find radiance in our dance.

Waves of Understanding

In the quiet moments found,
Waves wash upon the shore,
Gentle whispers of the sound,
Promises of something more.

Hearts adrift in endless seas,
Tides rise to meet the day,
Bound by currents, minds at ease,
Finding light in the spray.

With every crest, a story grows,
A dance beneath the sun,
In the depths, a truth that glows,
Unraveling, we've begun.

Connection finds a way to bloom,
In silence, we speak true,
Navigating through the gloom,
Together, we'll pull through.

As the horizon fades to night,
Stars emerge to guide our soul,
In the dark, we find our light,
Waves of love make us whole.

The Pulse of Connection

In crowded rooms, a spark ignites,
The heartbeat quickens, life abounds,
In every glance, a bond ignites,
A rhythm in our shared sounds.

Threads of laughter weave through space,
Unseen ties that pull us near,
In a smile, we find our grace,
A language spoken crystal clear.

With every heartbeat, stories blend,
Echoes of what's yet to come,
In this dance, we find a friend,
Together, we beat as one.

As moments pass, the pulse remains,
A melody that fills the air,
In joy and sorrow, love sustains,
This bond, we fiercely declare.

Through every change, we stay in tune,
A symphony of hearts aligned,
In the light of sun or moon,
The pulse of connection binds.

Threads Woven with Care

In the tapestry of this life,
Threads of moments intertwine,
Each connection stitches strife,
A pattern neither yours nor mine.

With love's touch, we weave our tales,
Colors bright and shadows deep,
Through storms that howl and wind that wails,
Together, promises we keep.

In the quiet, gently sewn,
Every laugh, a subtle hue,
Through the pain, seeds of love grown,
This fabric holds me close to you.

As we unravel, find the way,
To mend the fears that fray us still,
In every thread, a bright display,
Crafting solace with our will.

Together, we will always share,
In joy, in grief, we stand aware,
Through life's loom, we'll never tear,
Threads woven with enduring care.

Cadence of Companionship

In the rhythm of our days,
Friendship dances by your side,
In laughter, we find our ways,
A bond that cannot be denied.

With every step, we find the beat,
Two voices in a sweet refrain,
In harmony, our hearts repeat,
In sunshine or in pouring rain.

As seasons change, we hold our ground,
In trials, we find shared might,
In silence, comfort can be found,
In shadows, we ignite the light.

Through valleys low and mountains high,
Together, we begin anew,
With every heartbeat, reach the sky,
In every moment, deep and true.

So let us dance through life’s embrace,
In cadence, ever close we stand,
Forever moving, heart in place,
Companionship's a steady hand.

Harmonies of Connection

In whispered tones we find our way,
A melody that softly sways.
Each note a bond, each chord a tie,
Together we can touch the sky.

Through laughter shared and tears we shed,
In every word, the love we've bred.
Our hearts in sync, a blissful sound,
In this sweet dance, true joy is found.

The world may change, but we will stay,
In harmonies that guide our play.
A symphony of souls entwined,
In every rhythm, love defined.

With every heartbeat, we compose,
A timeless tale that gently flows.
In perfect tune, we rise and fall,
Together we can face it all.

So let us sing this song of grace,
In every moment, find our place.
In the harmonies that we create,
In connection deep, we celebrate.

Tides of Trust

The waves arrive, then gently flee,
A rhythm of what’s meant to be.
With each embrace, believe and see,
In tides of trust, we roam so free.

The shore may shift, the currents strong,
Yet here we stand, where we belong.
In safety found, we weave the song,
Through every storm, we still hold on.

Whenever doubts might cloud the skies,
Just look within, where truth resides.
In every glance, a promise lies,
Together, we are wise and wise.

As moonlight guides the sea at night,
In whispers shared, we find the light.
With every rise, a new delight,
Through tides of trust, we soar in flight.

So let the waves crash loud and bold,
With hearts entwined, our stories told.
In this embrace, we shall behold,
In tides of trust, our love is gold.

The Dance of Duo

Two bodies move as one in grace,
In every step, a sweet embrace.
With laughter bright and eyes aglow,
In rhythm found, we ebb and flow.

With every turn, the world does fade,
In this ballet, our fears cascade.
In perfect sync, the heartbeats play,
A timeless waltz where we shall stay.

Through whispered secrets and stolen looks,
Each moment writes the songs in books.
With every leap, horizons stretch,
In this duet, love finds its sketch.

Though storms may rise and shadows fall,
Together, we shall stand so tall.
In harmony, a bond so true,
In every dance, it's me and you.

So take my hand, the stage is set,
In every heartbeat, no regret.
In the dance of duo, hearts ignite,
In timeless motion, pure delight.

Tuning Forks of Emotion

In silent rooms, our hearts align,
Resonating like a string divine.
With gentle touch, we find the tone,
In tuning forks, we're never alone.

Each glance a spark, each sigh a wave,
In silent language, souls are brave.
Through emotional strains, we refine,
Our finest moments intertwined.

With empathy, we tune the air,
In every heartbeat, love laid bare.
With every note, our spirits soar,
In perfect pitch, we ask for more.

Though shadows creep and doubts may loom,
We strike the chord that lights the room.
In frail vibrations, strength we find,
With tuning forks that bind our mind.

So listen close to what we share,
In melodies that fill the air.
In perfect harmony, let it be,
In tuning forks, love sets us free.

Shadows of Sharing

In the quiet night, whispers blend,
Secrets and stories, paths that wend.
Flickering lights, shadows entwined,
Hearts in the dark, gently aligned.

A touch of laughter, a hand in hand,
Moments cherished, fragile yet grand.
Echoes of trust, softly they fall,
Building a bridge, uniting us all.

Through trials faced, we stand as one,
In the dance of life, shadows run.
Together we weave, from dusk till dawn,
Painting our dreams, as night turns to yawn.

With every heartbeat, we share our plight,
Finding our strength, in shared twilight.
Voices like candles, flicker and sway,
Guiding each other, lighting the way.

In shadows of sharing, bonds stay tight,
Creating our story, our shared light.
Together we rise, hand in hand,
In shadows of sharing, we boldly stand.

Dance of the Dreamers

In the realm of stars, whispers call,
Dreamers unite, beneath night's pall.
Feet on the ground, hearts in the sky,
Together they soar, as the moments fly.

A waltz of wishes, magic in air,
Spinning like leaves, without a care.
Eyes filled with wonder, souls set free,
Dancing through life, in sweet harmony.

Glimmers of hope, guiding the way,
In pockets of joy, where shadows play.
Stars framed in laughter, echo so high,
In the dance of dreamers, we were born to fly.

With every twirl, a memory made,
Hearts entwined like a gentle braid.
Through night's embrace, we sway and glide,
In the dance of dreamers, side by side.

Every step taken, a vision bold,
A tapestry woven, stories unfold.
In the realm of dreams, let love grow,
In the dance of dreamers, let spirits flow.

Tapestry of Trust

Threads interwoven in colors bright,
Stitch by stitch, we craft our light.
Each moment shared, a pattern unfolds,
In the tapestry of trust, love beholds.

Through the storms we face, and gentle gales,
We stand together, where trust prevails.
A hug, a smile, a knowing glance,
In the warmth of honesty, we learn to dance.

Together we mend, the frays of the past,
In this sacred bond, our shadows cast.
We build and we break, in patience and time,
Creating a rhythm, a sweet, simple rhyme.

A patchwork of laughter, tears in between,
Each thread a journey, together we glean.
Embracing the flaws, we wear them with pride,
In the tapestry of trust, with hearts open wide.

As the fabric glimmers with every hue,
Stories of friendship, steadfast and true.
In the quilt of life, let's weave our part,
A tapestry of trust, stitched from the heart.

Melodies of Memory

Soft notes drift, like whispers of time,
Echoes of laughter, a gentle chime.
Fading like shadows in the waning light,
Melodies linger, holding on tight.

In a crowded room, familiar songs play,
Bringing us back to those golden days.
Each note a reminder, a cherished thread,
Of moments together, and words left unsaid.

The symphony swells, as we close our eyes,
Painting our dreams in the vastest skies.
Footsteps together, in rhythm we tread,
Melodies echo where our hearts have led.

From whispers of childhood to whispers of love,
The music transcends, like stars up above.
With every refrain, our spirits take flight,
In the melodies of memory, we find our light.

So let the music forever play on,
For each note we cherish, never truly gone.
In the fabric of time, our songs will reside,
In the melodies of memory, right by our side.

The Pulse of Presence

In the quiet of the night,
Hearts beat soft and low,
A rhythm shared in silence,
Where thoughts begin to flow.

Moments stretch and linger,
As time begins to blend,
The pulse of gentle knowing,
In presence, we transcend.

Eyes that speak in whispers,
Holding stories untold,
In every glance exchanged,
A warmth against the cold.

Hands that brush like feathers,
In a dance both bold and shy,
Together we create,
A canvas of the sky.

In this sacred stillness,
Life's essence we embrace,
For in the pulse of presence,
We find our truest grace.

Flickers of Familiarity

In the corner of my eye,
A spark ignites the air,
Familiar laughter lingers,
A melody we share.

Through the haze of memories,
Echoes softly call,
Flickers of familiarity,
In the dance of it all.

In the stories woven tight,
Threads of love entwine,
Each glance a silent nod,
To the ties that align.

The warmth of shared embraces,
Fills the spaces unseen,
In the glow of old moments,
Past and present convene.

Though the world may shift around,
These sparks will never fade,
For in the heart of friendship,
A legacy is made.

The Symphony of Together

In harmony we gather,
Every note in tune,
The symphony of laughter,
Beneath the silver moon.

Strings entwine like lifelines,
Creating magic here,
In this orchestra of souls,
Resonating clear.

Chords that rise like whispers,
In the cool night air,
We compose our moments,
With a love that we share.

Every pause a heartbeat,
Every echo a sigh,
Together we are stronger,
In the sound of our why.

As the sun begins to break,
A new dawn's gentle glow,
The symphony of together,
Continues to flow.

Cadence of Companionship

Beneath the sprawling branches,
We found our secret place,
A cadence of companionship,
In nature's warm embrace.

With every step together,
Our laughter fills the air,
In the dance of friendship,
We find love everywhere.

As seasons shift and change,
Our hearts remain aligned,
In the cadence of our journey,
A bond uniquely designed.

Through storms and sunny days,
We weather every trial,
With every joyful moment,
We share a lasting smile.

In the echoes of tomorrow,
We'll carry what we've known,
For in the cadence of companionship,
We've truly found a home.

Harmonics in Harmony

In twilight's glow, the stars align,
Whispers of night, a sweet design.
Melodies dance through air so pure,
Hearts entwined in rhythms sure.

Soft echoes rise, a gentle stream,
Notes of hope, a shared dream.
Together we breathe, in sync we flow,
Harmonies bloom where love will grow.

Through valleys deep, our voices soar,
A symphony found on nature's floor.
With every beat, we chase the light,
Creating magic in the night.

Conversations in the Air

In gentle breezes, words take flight,
A dance of thoughts, both day and night.
Whispers carried on the wind,
Tales of joy and love unpinned.

Clouds may change, yet still we speak,
In winding paths, our hearts unique.
Shared laughter echoes, shadows play,
Moments cherished along the way.

Secrets linger like the dew,
In every glance, a bond anew.
The air is thick with unvoiced dreams,
As silence buzzes with hopeful schemes.

A Journey of Two

Beneath the stars, our paths entwine,
Each whispered wish, a sacred sign.
Through winding roads, our hearts align,
A journey shared, both yours and mine.

Mountains rise, and rivers flow,
Together we face what's yet to show.
In every step, a story grows,
In laughter loud, in soft echoes.

With hands held tight, we brave the storm,
In every challenge, our hearts keep warm.
Together we write this tale so true,
A journey crafted for me and you.

Love's Gentle Murmurs

In twilight’s hush, our hearts entwine,
Soft whispers float on fragrant pine.
Every gaze, a silent song,
In love's embrace, where we belong.

Blushing skies and fading light,
In quiet moments, our souls unite.
Gentle murmurs brush the air,
With tender sighs, we lay our bare.

As moonlight spills on silver seas,
Your laughter dances with the breeze.
Through whispered dreams, we softly sway,
In love's gentle murmur, we find our way.

Embracing Echoes

Whispers dance in quiet night,
Carried soft on gentle light.
Memories linger, hearts align,
In the silence, love will shine.

Every sound a story told,
Through the years, both young and old.
Each echo forms a sacred bond,
In every heartbeat, we respond.

Footsteps trace the paths we share,
In the moments, we declare.
Embracing echoes, side by side,
In unity, our hopes abide.

Through valleys deep and mountains high,
Voices rise and softly sigh.
Together facing all we meet,
In every challenge, we are sweet.

As stars align in twilight's glow,
We find the love we always know.
In each echo, a promise made,
In the silence, we are laid.

Synchronizing Souls

Hearts entwined in rhythmic beat,
In this dance, we find our seat.
Every glance, a spark ignites,
Synchronizing through the nights.

Through the chaos, we will flow,
Learning secrets love can show.
In the quiet, we find peace,
In this bond, our fears release.

With each step, we share the weight,
Trusting time won't separate.
In the music, we will soar,
Synchronizing evermore.

Looking deep into your eyes,
I see truth beneath the lies.
In this moment, still and whole,
Two together, one pure soul.

When the world feels heavy, cold,
In your warmth, I am consoled.
Hand in hand, forever near,
Together, we can face our fear.

Vibration of Voices

In the crowd, we find our song,
A tapestry where we belong.
With every shout, a life we save,
A vibration strong, our hearts behave.

Words like pulses, share the air,
In this rhythm, we lay bare.
Echoes rise, the chorus swells,
In every note, our spirit dwells.

Together forming waves of sound,
In our unity, love is found.
Every heartbeat sings the truth,
In the noise, we find our youth.

Resonating through the night,
Voices merging, pure delight.
With every whisper, every cheer,
We create a world so dear.

As we gather, fear will fade,
In this bond, our lives are laid.
A vibration strong, we will rise,
In our voices, the future lies.

Constellations of Care

Stars above, a canvas bright,
Guiding souls through endless night.
In the dark, we find our way,
Constellations here to stay.

Each sparkle tells a tale of love,
Woven threads from skies above.
In our hearts, the lights we bear,
Illuminating all we share.

Through the trials, we remain,
In this journey, joy and pain.
Connected by the dreams we weave,
In constellations, we believe.

With every breath, a wish we make,
In the night, our spirits wake.
Hand in hand, we soar on air,
Creating paths with tender care.

In the universe, we find our place,
In this dance, a warm embrace.
Guiding lights and gentle stars,
In constellations, healing scars.

Resonating Promises

In whispers soft, we make our vows,
Underneath the silent stars,
Each promise glows, a guiding light,
Through shadowed paths and endless trials.

Your heartbeat syncs with mine at dusk,
A melody that never fades,
In every glance, a tale unfolds,
Resonating through the years.

With every dream, we build anew,
Foundations crafted in trust's warm glow,
Together facing the unknown,
A journey forged in love's embrace.

Through storms that rage and skies that clear,
We stand as one, unyielding strength,
And in the silence, hear the truth,
Our promises, a bond unbreakable.

Forever etched in heart and soul,
A symphony of us, divine,
Through every shadow, every light,
Resonating, our love aligns.

The Anatomy of Us

In tender smiles, our story breathes,
A rhythm found in shared heartbeats,
Your hand in mine, a map of dreams,
The anatomy of what love means.

With laughter laced in gentle eyes,
We paint our world, blue, bright skies,
Moments captured, a fleeting sigh,
In the tapestry of you and I.

Each secret whispered in the dark,
A spark igniting in the park,
Threads of memories intertwine,
Creating patterns all divine.

Through trials faced, we grow and learn,
In every twist, a fire burns,
The fibers strong, yet soft to touch,
The anatomy of us, a perfect clutch.

In every heartbeat, every glance,
We find our way, a timeless dance,
Together, whole, we rise above,
In every layer, we find our love.

Flickers of Bonding

In quiet nights, the stars ignite,
Flickers of bonding fill the skies,
With laughter shared and secrets told,
A warmth that wraps, a love so bold.

Through fleeting glances, hearts align,
In every step, your hand in mine,
Moments spark like fireflies,
Illuminating the darkest skies.

With every smile, a story starts,
A canvas painted with our hearts,
In the stillness, our spirits soar,
Flickers of bonding at our core.

In whispered words beneath the moon,
A symphony that ends too soon,
Yet in the dawn, it comes alive,
Flickers of love that always thrive.

As seasons change, we find our way,
Together facing each new day,
In fragile moments, fierce and bright,
Flickers of bonding, pure delight.

Interludes of Togetherness

In quiet moments, time suspends,
Interludes where our hearts blend,
Each laugh, a note in life's sweet song,
Together, where we both belong.

Through gentle whispers, soft and light,
We share our hopes, our dreams in flight,
In every glance, a story told,
Interludes of love, brave and bold.

With each embrace, the world fades out,
In cozy corners, there's no doubt,
Together, we build our sacred space,
Interludes of joy, a warm embrace.

Through trials faced, we stand as one,
In every battle, we've already won,
With open hearts, we pave the way,
Interludes of trust, come what may.

In every heartbeat, every sigh,
The echoes of you and I,
Together, painted in vibrant hues,
Interludes of us, forever true.

Unraveled Bonds

In quiet whispers, trust unwinds,
Threads of connection softly break.
What once was strong, now it finds,
A path unwayed, a silent ache.

Memories linger, frayed at seams,
Like faded photos lost in time.
We walked together in shared dreams,
Now shadows drift, a haunting rhyme.

The laughter echoes, bittersweet,
In corners where we used to play.
Yet, time has thrown us to our feet,
A journey lost, a winding way.

Yet still I hold a glimmer bright,
Of moments cherished, flames aglow.
Each smile, each tear, a guiding light,
In our hearts, the love still flows.

Though bonds may fray and paths diverge,
A piece of you will always stay.
In whispered winds, our memories surge,
Unraveled, yes, but never stray.

Reflections of Us

In the mirror, our shadows dance,
Faint echoes of laughter resound.
Every glance, a fleeting chance,
To trace the love that we have found.

Time weaves dreams upon our skin,
Worn edges tell tales of our plight.
Through tangled thorns, we learned to win,
Each battle fought, ignited light.

In quiet moments, whispers call,
A symphony of souls entwined.
Together we rise, together we fall,
With every heartbeat, love defined.

Reflections fade, yet still remain,
Like footprints left upon the shore.
Our essence lingers, soft as rain,
In every breath, forevermore.

So let the world turn, vast and wide,
With you, I stand, my heart will trust.
For in this life, we've carved our stride,
Two souls as one, reflections of us.

The Music of Moments

In twilight's hush, the melody starts,
Soft notes drift on a gentle breeze.
A symphony plays, weaving our hearts,
Each moment captured, time's sweet tease.

Laughter lingers, a fragile sound,
Dancing lightly on the air.
With every glance, love does rebound,
An orchestra of dreams laid bare.

Through seasons change, the rhythm flows,
A timeless waltz beneath the stars.
With every beat, affection grows,
In shared silence, healing scars.

Each touch, a note in life's refrain,
The echoes of our story shared.
In the music, joy and pain,
Together, unafraid and bared.

Let's dance forever, stars align,
In this sweet concert of embrace.
For in the music, we find the sign,
Of moments cherished, love's true grace.

Interwoven Souls

Threads of fate in colors bright,
Intertwined, our stories blend.
In the tapestry of night,
Two hearts entwined, a steadfast friend.

Weaving dreams in hushed delight,
Each strand a whisper in the dark.
Through every storm, we share the light,
Guided by love, a steady spark.

In the fabric of time, we belong,
Patterns formed with care and grace.
An echo of a sacred song,
In every stitch, your warm embrace.

Though miles may stretch and worlds may change,
The fibers hold our bond secure.
In tangled paths, we may feel strange,
Yet through it all, our love is pure.

So here we stand, our hearts in tow,
Interwoven souls, forever bold.
In the daylight's glow, through night's soft glow,
Our story's warmth will never fold.

The Melody of Moments

In the hush of twilight glow,
Whispers of time start to flow,
Notes of laughter softly play,
Crafting memories of the day.

A dance of shadows, light and shade,
Echoes in the glen we made,
Melodies linger, sweet and clear,
Filling our hearts with joy and cheer.

With every heartbeat, a new refrain,
Stories braided in joy and pain,
Time's gentle hands guide us so,
Through every pulse, the moments grow.

A symphony of souls entwined,
Harmony that fate has designed,
Through each crescendo, love we find,
Binding the threads of the kind.

As evening falls, the stars will gleam,
Weaving dreams in one great seam,
In the silence, united we are,
Singing a song beneath the star.

Pulse of Togetherness

In the dance of evening light,
Hearts beat gently, close and tight,
Every smile, a shared embrace,
Filling the world with warmth and grace.

Colors blend in twilight's art,
Every moment, a brand new start,
With hands held firm, we walk as one,
Chasing dreams beneath the sun.

In laughter’s echo, joy we find,
A melody that’s truly blind,
Across the distance, love won’t part,
For every pulse beats in the heart.

Through storms and trials, we will stand,
An unbroken line, a guiding hand,
Together we’ll weave our stories true,
In the rhythm of me and you.

As seasons change and time moves on,
The pulse of love will never be gone,
With every beat, together we’ll sway,
In the embrace of every day.

The Light in You and Me

In the quiet dawn, we rise,
Chasing dreams beneath bright skies,
You and I, two flames so free,
Sparkling light for all to see.

With every step, we chase the fire,
Filling the world with our desire,
In your eyes, I see the glow,
A warmth that only love can show.

As shadows fade and moments blend,
Together we rise, time won't end,
Hand in hand, we'll find our way,
Lighting paths for each new day.

Through laughter shared and tears we shed,
A bond unbroken, gently spread,
In the light that shines from you,
A guiding star to lead us through.

With every heartbeat, a spark ignites,
In the dark, we find the sights,
For in the light of you and me,
A universe awaits, wild and free.

Winds of Wisdom

In the garden where we stand,
Gentle breezes kiss the land,
Whispers echo through the trees,
In every rustle, hidden keys.

Clouds drift softly, tales to tell,
Nature's secrets ringing well,
With every gust, a lesson flows,
In the wind, true wisdom grows.

Through valleys deep and mountains tall,
Voices call, and shadows fall,
Listening closely, hearts can hear,
The ancient truths that draw us near.

In the dance of leaves and air,
We find a path, a bond to share,
For in the currents, we may see,
The strength found in harmony.

As night falls and stars appear,
The winds of wisdom draw us near,
With open hearts, let's trust the way,
For in the breeze, we learn to sway.

Milton Keynes UK
Ingram Content Group UK Ltd.
UKHW020816061124
450821UK00012B/689

9 789916 868010